J is for JUSTIFY

Written and Illustrated by Lesley A.J. Baumann

Published by Alizarin Chestnut
www.alizarinchestnut.com

Published by Alizarin Chestnut
Dayton, Ohio
www.alizarinchestnut.com

First Edition, May 2019
ISBN 978-1-7339264-0-9
Library of Congress Control Number: 2019938964

Printed in Korea by Four Colour Print Group, Louisville, Kentucky.

JisforJustify.com

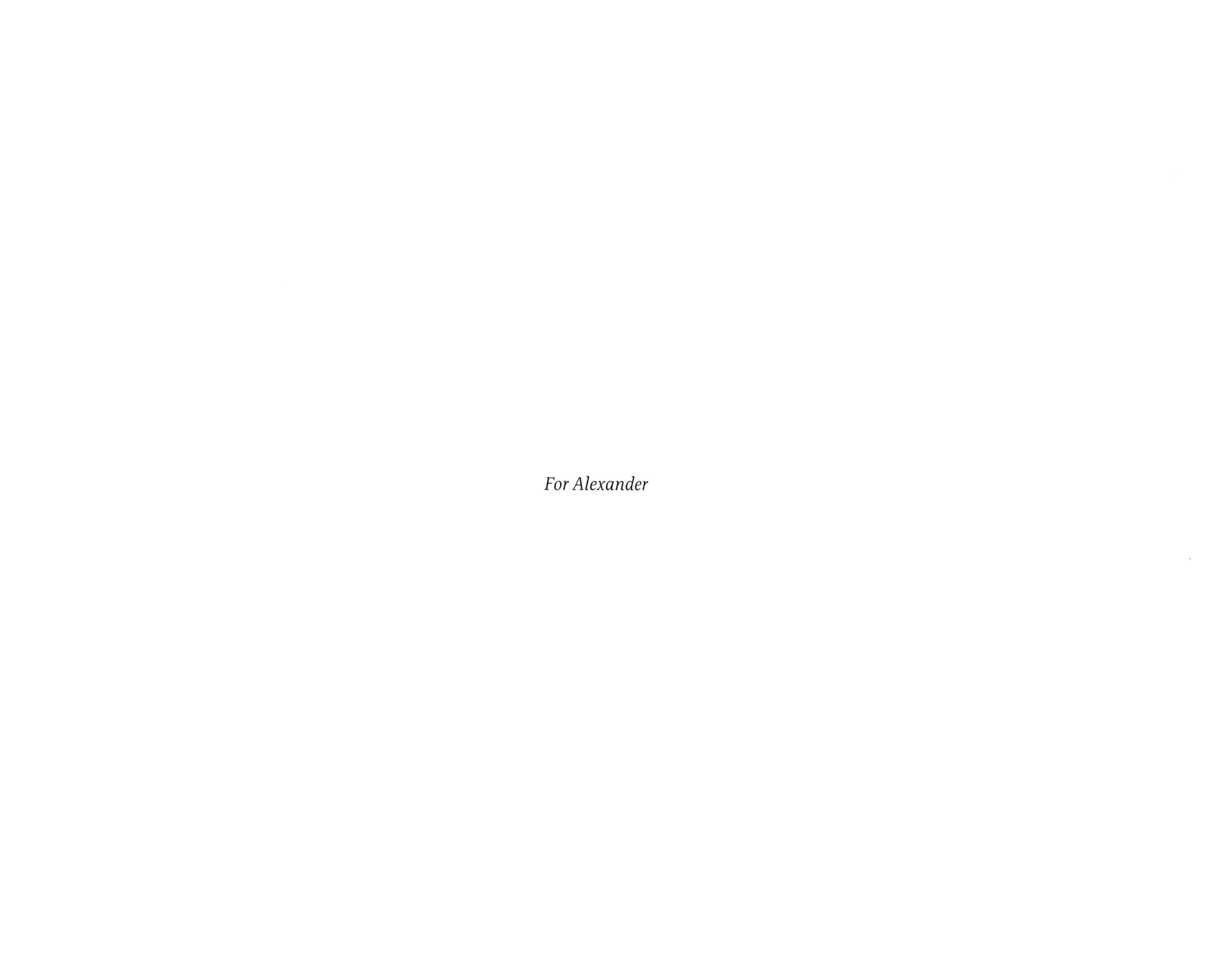

For Alexander

A

American Pharoah

American Pharoah was born one chilly Groundhog Day.
Three years later he ran for the roses on the first Saturday in May.
The word "Pharaoh" in his name was actually misspelled;
but, thanks to his long stride on the track, he truly excelled.
This bay with a faint star was as gentle as a lamb.
He went on to win Thoroughbred racing's first Grand Slam.

A

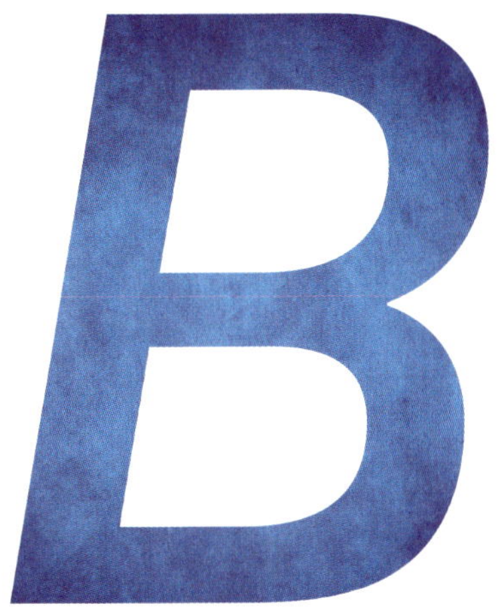

Barbaro

This handsome bay won the Derby in spectacular fashion.
And, after his Preakness injury, the world demonstrated such compassion.
For months fans watched for news of his recovery in the headlines,
and donations in his memory have advanced veterinary medicine for equines.
A statue at Churchill Downs depicts one of his most memorable poses,
while buried underneath he must surely dream of roses.

B

Citation

Time and time again "Big Cy" demonstrated consistence.
He could win on any track at any distance.
He was owned and bred by Calumet.
He often traveled by rail, but his name inspired that of a jet.
His owner had a stipulation to declare,
and so Citation raced until he was a millionaire.

C

Dr. Fager

Dr. Charles Anthony Fager was his namesake,
and zoos concluded that he could leave cheetahs in his wake.
He once won four titles in a single season,
and any horse who looked him in the eye was beaten.
While Dr. Fager was amazingly versatile,
he's best known for setting the world record at a mile.

D

Easy Goer

He and Sunday Silence had a great rivalry on the track.
In the Kentucky Derby, the black colt beat him to the head of the pack.
Their clash at Pimlico is regarded as the most exciting Preakness ever.
For Sunday Silence, it was another successful endeavor.
With the Triple Crown at stake, fans watched from sea to sea.
But, this time Easy Goer proved the Belmont was his cup of tea.

E

F Forego

This big, ornery bay would stare down his competition.
Getting to the finish line first was his mission.
They loaded him down with enough weight to stop a freight train,
but that did little to keep him out of the fast lane.
With courage and heart, this superstar left his mark.
In his retirement fans flocked to visit him at the Kentucky Horse Park.

F

Gallant Fox

The great “Sunny Jim” Fitzsimmons was his trainer,
and with great victories each of them became a Hall of Famer.
For his three-year-old season, jockey Earl Sande came out of retirement.
Together they won what was then known as the “Triple Event.”
This gallant bay was often referred to as the “Fox of Belair.”
His crowning accomplishment was something he and his son would share.

G

Holy Bull

"The Bull" was a striking dapple gray.
He was best known for his courage at the end of the day.
Aggressive on the track, he might bite his foes.
Off the track, he was known to spot photographers and kindly strike a pose.
He could win a race at any distance with his extreme acceleration.
In his thrilling Travers victory, he held off a charge with great determination.

H

I'll Have Another

When it came to cookies, this chestnut's owner loved to have one more.
Out on the track, I'll Have Another was lucky to have Lava Man as a mentor.
Roses were bestowed upon this racing machine
after he became the first horse to win the Derby from post nineteen.
After winning the Preakness, his racing career met the end of its span.
He eventually went to live in California after spending some time in Japan.

J

Unraced at two, before the Derby he had little time to rehearse.
Nonetheless he won the race and broke Apollo's Curse.
His victorious emergence from the Preakness fog was quite serene.
Next he won the Belmont and Triple Crown thirteen.
He had exploded onto the scene and defied expectation.
He proved that you should dare to dream and captured our imagination.

KC
J

K

Kelso

Sired by Your Host, he had such courage, consistency and drive.
He won Horse of the Year not two or three times but five.
Successful for so many seasons, horses like him are now obsolete.
When he finally retired, he enjoyed his days with a pony named Pete.
Throughout his career this son of Maid of Flight had run like he had wings.
Now his gravestone in Maryland reads, "Where he gallops, the earth sings."

K

L

Lava Man

The most successful claimer in history, he won on both turf and dirt.
This attention-loving gelding was quite the extrovert.
When he didn't take to retirement, his trainer tried another approach.
Lava Man began his second career and became known as "Coach."
Though behind him were his days as a runner,
on Derby Day he was the lead pony for I'll Have Another.

Man o' War

As he ran with ease, many world, track and stakes records were set.
His name is one that racing fans will never forget.
He was loved by his groom who declared him the "Mostest Hoss,"
and his defeat by Upset was his only loss.
At an incredible 28 feet, he had the world's longest stride.
His best friend, a calm hunter named Major Treat, was often by his side.

M

Native Dancer

This early sports superstar was known as the "Gray Ghost."
His reputation was one that television helped build from coast to coast.
His silks were cerise with white diamonds, and his coat was dapple gray,
He only had one bad race — unfortunately it was on Derby Day.
He was strong-willed and loved to come from behind,
and in his stall he hung out with kittens to unwind.

Omaha

He was the son of one of racing's Triple Crown winning elite,
and the "Belair Bullet" went on to match his father's feat.
He demonstrated great speed and stamina while in motion,
and he was the first Triple Crown winner to compete across the ocean.
Omaha retired to the town in Nebraska whose name he bore.
There he spent his days with a groom whom he had such a rapport.

P

Point Given

When the "Big Red Train" ran, he was poetry in motion.
On the track in the mornings, this clown loved to cause commotion.
He was really good at raking in the dough —
he became the first horse to win four million-dollar races in a row.
He retired to the Kentucky Horse Park's Hall of Champions
where fans love to visit and wish him congratulations.

P

Quiet American

This grandson of Dr. Fager was bred in the Sunshine State.
Lightly raced at ages two and three, at four he began to captivate.
Steadfast on the track, he raced determinedly to the wire.
He then went on to become a champion sire.
He lived a long, happy life dying at age thirty.
His most famous son, Real Quiet, won the Kentucky Derby.

Q

Rachel Alexandra

This famous filly blew away the field in the Kentucky Oaks.
Her courage and grace endeared her to many folks.
Next she ran in the Preakness where she continued to make noise.
She became the first filly in 85 years to win it against the boys.
After her historic Woodward victory, you wouldn't believe the jubilation at the "Spa."
Her Horse of the Year title, the first for a 3-year-old female, continues to inspire awe.

R

Secretariat

"Big Red" is one of the most famous racehorses in the land.
To this day, his records in the Triple Crown races still stand.
His great stamina and efficient stride were among his strengths.
He won the Belmont by an astonishing 31 lengths!
His record-breaking syndication was a cultural force,
and they discovered his heart was twice the size of a normal horse.

S

T

Tiznow

A leg injury led to the late start of his career,
but he would go on to inspire others by his ability to persevere.
He had a blaze on his face shaped like a tornado,
and he was the first horse to win the Breeders' Cup Classic twice in a row.
While on the track, he was determined and gritty,
but in the barn his tricks were rather witty.

T

Unbridled

On television he had an unforgettable Kentucky Derby win.
We got to see his owner's reaction — she had quite the grin.
He had an ongoing rivalry with a horse named Summer Squall.
Against a Breeders Cup Classic field of champs, he beat them all.
While Dr. Fager is a name in his family tree,
Unbridled also appears in American Pharoah's pedigree.

V

Some of the names in his pedigree are downright crazy.
Thank goodness he didn't take after his dam who was named Lazy!
In the second running of the Kentucky Derby he faced his rival, Parole.
Like two of his brothers who aimed to win this race, he accomplished his goal.
After his racing career, pulling a vegetable cart must have been lame,
but then he became a saddle horse for a Long Island lady since he was so tame.

V

War Admiral

While he didn't inherit the looks of his sire,
he most certainly acquired Man o' War's fire.
Against starting gates, he was ever on the attack.
During the Great Depression, fans looked forward to seeing him on the track.
"The Admiral" was the fourth Triple Crown winner and one of racing's exemplary,
but he lost to Seabiscuit in the "Match Race of the Century."

W

X

Xtra Heat

This bay lady was a daughter of Louisiana Derby winner Dixieland Heat.
On the track she was a sprinter that was tough to beat.
Though these shorter distances best suited her ability,
she was presented the Eclipse Award for overall Three-Year-Old Filly.
Her consistency lead to her acclaim,
and she was later inducted to the Hall of Fame.

X

Y

Your Host

Known as the "Magnificent Cripple" even before his big wreck,
this horse was born with a crooked eye, ear and neck.
Four white leg markings are bad luck according to superstition.
Could that be why he broke his leg and his shoulder in a racing collision?
He demonstrated incredible courage in the recovery he had to undergo.
Your Host went on to sire the great Kelso.

Y

Z

Zenyatta

Fans admired the way their beloved "Queen Z" would prance.
Their favorite part of her prerace routine was that dance.
She preferred to stare at her competition rather than warm up
and became the first female to win the Classic in the Breeders' Cup.
Zenyatta went on quite an epic winning spree
that didn't end until her nineteenth consecutive victory.

Z

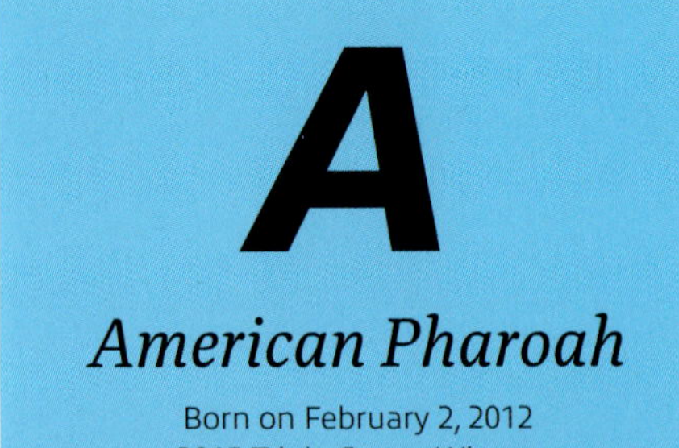

A

American Pharoah

Born on February 2, 2012
2015 Triple Crown Winner

B

Barbaro

Born on April 29, 2003
2006 Kentucky Derby Winner

C

Citation

Born on April 11, 1945
1948 Triple Crown Winner

D

Dr. Fager

Born on April 6, 1964

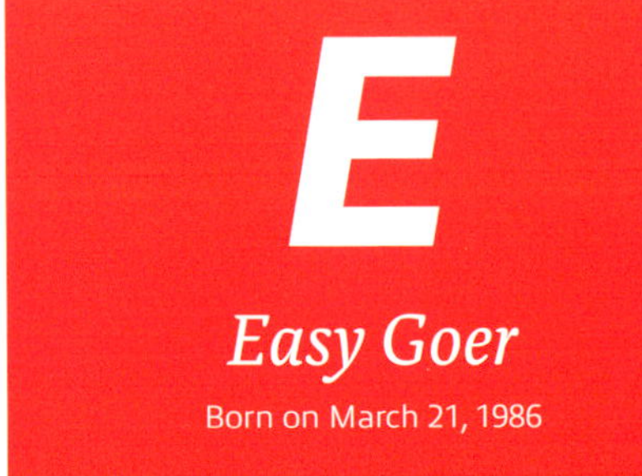

E

Easy Goer

Born on March 21, 1986

F

Forego

Born on April 30, 1970

G

Gallant Fox

Born on March 23, 1927
1930 Triple Crown Winner

H

Holy Bull

Born on January 24, 1991

I

I'll Have Another

Born on April 1, 2009
2012 Kentucky Derby Winner

J

Justify

Born on March 28, 2015
2018 Triple Crown Winner

K

Kelso

Born on April 4, 1957

L

Lava Man

Born on March 20, 2001

M

Man o' War

Born on March 29, 1917

N

Native Dancer

Born on March 27, 1950

O

Omaha

Born on March 24, 1932
1935 Triple Crown Winner

P

Point Given

Born on March 27, 1998

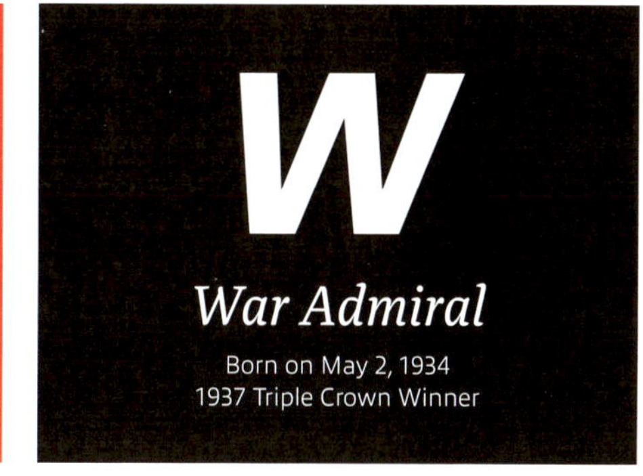

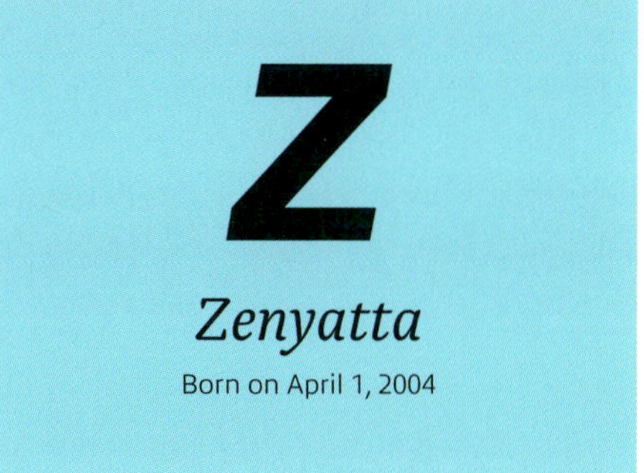

*Thoroughbreds share a universal birthday of January 1st. This helps ease any confusion when entering horses in races which are restricted to specific age groups.

Glossary

Apollo's Curse – No horse since Apollo had been able to win the Kentucky Derby without racing as a two-year-old first for 136 years until Justify was able to do it again.

Bay – A brown colored horse with a black mane, tail, lower legs and tips of ears.

Belmont – The Belmont Stakes is the third race in the Triple Crown series. It is 1 ½ miles in distance and held every June at Belmont Park. It is open to three-year-old colts and fillies.

Blaze – A wide, white marking that extends most of the length of a horse's face.

Breeders' Cup – An annual series of year-end world championship races for Thoroughbreds around the world. It is held in North America at a different track each year.

Breeders' Cup Classic – This 1¼ mile race is the richest of all the Breeder's Cup events. It is open to horses ages 3 years and up.

Cerise – A vivid, pinkish-red color.

Chestnut – A reddish-brown colored horse.

Churchill Downs – The racetrack in Louisville, Kentucky, where the Kentucky Derby is held.

Claimer – A horse that was acquired in a claiming race, a race in which all of the horses are for sale.

Colt – A young, male horse.

Dam – A horse's mother.

Dapple Gray – A gray horse with lighter spots throughout its coat.

Eclipse Awards – Named for a famous stallion, these American Thoroughbred racing awards are given to people and horses in a number of categories after the end of the year.

Equine – This is another word for horse and is often used to describe things relating to horses.

Filly – A young, female horse.

Gelding – A castrated male.

Grand Slam of Thoroughbred Racing – Winning all three of the Triple Crown races and the Breeders' Cup Classic.

Great Depression – An economic crisis that hit the world in the 1930s. Many people had a hard time finding jobs and paying for food during this time. Horse racing was often a welcomed distraction that lifted their spirits.

Groom – A person who takes care of horses.

Hall of Fame – The National Racing Museum and Hall of Fame is located in Saratoga Springs, New York, and recognizes exceptional horses, trainers and jockeys.

Horse of the Year – The Eclipse Award for the overall most outstanding horse of the past year.

Kentucky Derby – The Kentucky Derby is one of the most famous races in the world and the first race in the Triple Crown series. It is 1¼ miles in distance and held on the first Saturday of every May at Churchill Downs. It is open to three-year-old colts and fillies.

Kentucky Horse Park – Located in Lexington, Kentucky, this park is the combination of a working farm, an educational attraction and an event facility.

Kentucky Oaks – This premier race for three-year-old fillies is held every year at Churchill Downs on the day before the Kentucky Derby.

Mare – An adult, female horse.

Match Race of the Century – This special race was arranged for Seabiscuit and War Admiral during the Great Depression at Pimlico Race Course.

Pedigree – A chart showing an individual horse's ancestors.

Pimlico Race Course – The track in Baltimore, Maryland, where the Preakness is held.

Pony – A full-sized horse used by a rider to lead a race horse on the track.

Post Position – The particular numbered stall in the starting gate assigned to a horse.

Preakness – The Preakness Stakes is the second race in the Triple Crown series. It is 1 ⅛ miles in distance and held every May at Pimlico Race Course. It is open to three-year-old colts and fillies.

Sire – A horse's father.

Spa – The nickname of Saratoga Race Course in Saratoga Springs, New York. The area is home to numerous mineral springs.

Stallion – An adult, male horse.

Star – A small, white marking on the forehead of a horse.

Starting Gate – A set of stalls whose doors fly open and signal the start of a horse race.

Stride – The distance a horse covers in one complete cycle of leg movements.

Sunshine State – The official nickname of the state of Florida.

Syndication – The selling of shares of a horse resulting in a large group of owners.

Thoroughbred – A breed of horse known for its use in racing. All of the horses in this book are Thoroughbreds.

Travers – The Travers Stakes is race for three-year-olds that is run at Saratoga Race Course and is often referred to as the "Midsummer Derby."

Triple Crown – The title awarded to a horse that wins the Kentucky Derby, the Preakness and the Belmont.

Woodward – The Woodward Stakes is a race for Thoroughbreds aged three years and up. Though it has been run at two other New York tracks in the past, it is now run at Saratoga Race Course.

The following two symbols are used throughout this book to recognize horses' extraordinary achievements.

 **Kentucky Derby Winner**

 **Triple Crown Winner**